■SCHOLAS

Money Math Learning Centers

10 Easy Centers With Skill-Building Activities That Teach Counting, One-to-One Correspondence, Sorting, Addition, and Subtraction—and Meet the NCTM Standards

by Shirley Barulich

NEW YORK • TORONTO • LONDON • AUCKLAND • SYDNEY

MEXICO CITY • NEW DELHI • HONG KONG • BUENOS AIRES

Teaching *Resources*

Dedication
To my mother and father

Acknowledgments
Thank you to my family, especially my husband, Robert,
for the support you gave me while I was writing this book

To all teachers—
The very best to you as you venture to give your students
an education that is taught in a meaningful way!

Cover design by Jason Robinson
Cover illustrations by Jackie Snider
Interior design by Russell Bart
Interior illustrations by Cary Pillo

ISBN 0-439-51381-2
Copyright © 2005 by Shirley Barulich
All rights reserved.
Printed in the U.S.A.

4 5 6 7 8 9 10   40   12 11 10 09 08 07

Contents

Money Math Learning Centers

Education, in an active meaningful context, will INSPIRE children to learn!

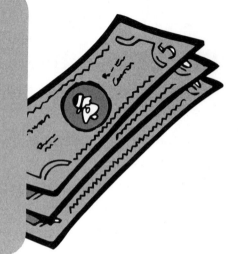

WE REMEMBER:

10 percent of what we read;

20 percent of what we hear;

30 percent of what we see;

50 percent of what we hear and see;

70 percent of what we say;

90 percent of what we say and do.

I am dedicated to the idea that children stay excited about learning when they can learn in an active way!

–Shirley Barulich

Welcome to *Money Math Learning Centers*!

What, you may ask, are "money math learning centers"? They are classroom-tested learning centers based on real-life establishments—the grocery, post office, clothing store, restaurant, and so on—that children are likely to encounter in their day-to-day lives. Because these centers closely relate to their own life experiences, children are highly motivated to learn from them. As they help set up and then "play pretend" in these centers, children will build essential math skills, such as money recognition, number recognition, counting, sorting, graphing, one-to-one correspondence, addition, subtraction, and more. (To find out how these centers correlate to the National Council of Teachers of Mathematics [NCTM] standards, see page 8.) They also build important language skills, such as writing and communicating with one another.

What's Inside?

In this book, you'll find everything you need to set up 10 super-fun money math learning centers in your classroom. For each center, you'll find:

- a list of math and other skills that children will learn as they engage in the center;
- a list of materials you'll need to set up the center;
- a reproducible note to parents that explains what children will be learning at the center and, if necessary, requests for items needed for the center;
- discussion questions that get children excited and motivated about the center;
- suggestions on how to set up the center with children's help;
- ideas for activities children can engage in while at the center;
- enrichment activities that enhance center time;
- literature links that relate to the theme; and
- reproducible pages that supplement the activities.

Making the Most of Center Time

- Before setting up a center, initiate a discussion with children to introduce them to the center. Use the questions provided as a starting point, then open up the discussion to give you a better idea of children's conceptual understanding and to give them an opportunity to inform and learn from one another.
- When setting up a center, incorporate children's ideas as much as possible. This gives them a sense of ownership in the learning process.
- In most centers, items will have to be sorted, labeled, and priced—a great opportunity to develop children's reasoning and writing skills, as well as promote cooperative learning.
- Allot about 30 minutes for center time. Depending on the size of your classroom or center, decide how many children will participate in the center at a time. (You may want to limit the number of participants to 8 at a time.) In most of the centers, you'll need to assign two children to be SELLERS—one child to collect money, the other to bag items. The rest can be SHOPPERS, who buy the items. (See "Pricing & Payment Methods," next page.) Rotate roles.
- While some children are at the center, make sure the rest of the class is engaged in self-directed, independent activities.
- If possible, take children on a related field trip. For example, if you're doing the Grocery Store center, take children to the neighborhood grocery store. Or, invite a grocer to talk about his or her job.
- Supplement each center with cross-curricular activities in literature, music, and art.

Pricing & Payment Methods

In many centers, you may want to ask children for suggestions on how much to price different items. Decide beforehand what money concepts you wish them to learn or review. Then give children a pricing range or specific amounts to use. For example, you might decide children will use pennies at the Best Books Store center and that prices will range from 1 to 10 cents.

Use one of the following options for pricing:

1) Label each item with pictures of the coins needed to pay for it. (See pages 12–13 for money art.) A shopper pays using those coins.

2) Write the amount of specific coins on the item. For example, 1¢ for a penny, 5¢ for a nickel, 10¢ for a dime, and so on.

3) For more advanced students, put a price that requires the use of a combination of coins. For example, if an item is 12¢, a shopper could pay with a dime and two pennies, or two nickels and two pennies, or twelve pennies.

Shoppers can pay for their purchases with play money, which is readily available in teacher stores or toy stores. You can also photocopy the money art on pages 12–13 on cardstock, cut them apart, have children color them, and then use them for currency.

You can also boost children's writing and math skills by asking them to use the payment forms on pages 14–16 when shopping. To use the payment forms, shoppers write the name of the item(s) they're buying, then write or color in the coins to show how much each item costs. Have children complete their payment forms at their desks. They can then take their item(s), completed payment form, and money to the cash register. One seller collects the payment form and money, while the other bags the item(s). If there's still time, shoppers can return and shop again!

At the End of Center Time

Before center time is over, make sure children have an opportunity to count how much they've collected. Here are a couple of options for counting money:

1) To count pennies (count by ones), have children place the pennies on a Hundred Board (you can get a plastic Hundred Board with raised grid to hold pennies in a school supply store). When the Hundred Board is filled, have children put the 100 pennies in a paper or plastic cup labeled "1 Dollar." Repeat this counting process until all the pennies have been counted.

2) For other coin denominations, use the Counting Number Lines on pages 10–11. For example, when counting dimes use the "Counting by Tens" number line, which goes up to 100 (10 dimes). When children have a dollar's worth of dimes, have them put the dimes in a cup labeled "1 Dollar."

When children have counted all the money in the register, have them write the amount in a cash-register receipt like the one below.

Date: June 6

Amount Received:
$1.50

Ways to Adapt Math Content

The math content suggested for each center is provided as a general guide. You can easily modify these ideas to meet children's needs by:

• using higher or lower prices.

• using a shopping list.

• giving children math problems related to the learning center before they start working in it.

• putting children on a "budget"—limit the amount of money they can spend at the center.

• asking children to total the prices of a group of items they're planning to buy.

• having children make change with the money they use and write it out as a math problem.

• asking children to draw or write about the graphs for the graphing activities in their journals. Pose questions to help children interpret the graphs. For example, how many is one part of the graph? Is this part more than/less than/equal to another part of the graph? How many more or less?

Meeting the NCTM Standards

	Number and Operations	Estimation*	Number Sense and Numeration	Concepts of Whole Number Numeration*	Whole Number Computation	Number Computation Operation*	Algebra (Patterns)	Geometry	Measurement	Data Analysis and Probability	Problem Solving	Reasoning and Proof	Communication	Connections	Representation
Best Books Store	✓	✓	✓	✓	✓				✓	✓	✓	✓	✓	✓	✓
Teddy Bear Clothing Store	✓		✓	✓	✓				✓	✓	✓	✓	✓	✓	✓
Rent-a-Pet Shop	✓	✓	✓	✓	✓				✓	✓	✓	✓	✓	✓	✓
Gift Shop	✓	✓	✓	✓		✓			✓	✓	✓	✓	✓	✓	✓
Grocery Store	✓		✓	✓	✓	✓			✓	✓	✓	✓	✓	✓	✓
Post Office	✓		✓	✓					✓		✓	✓	✓	✓	✓
Super Sticker Store	✓		✓	✓	✓				✓	✓	✓	✓	✓	✓	✓
Flower Shop	✓		✓	✓	✓				✓	✓	✓	✓	✓		✓
Lemonade Stand	✓	✓	✓	✓	✓					✓	✓	✓	✓	✓	✓
It's a Small World Eatery	✓		✓	✓	✓				✓	✓	✓	✓	✓	✓	✓

*Part of Number and Operations

Hundred Board

1	2	3	4	5	6	7	8	9	10
11	12	13	14	15	16	17	18	19	20
21	22	23	24	25	26	27	28	29	30
31	32	33	34	35	36	37	38	39	40
41	42	43	44	45	46	47	48	49	50
51	52	53	54	55	56	57	58	59	60
61	62	63	64	65	66	67	68	69	70
71	72	73	74	75	76	77	78	79	80
81	82	83	84	85	86	87	88	89	90
91	92	93	94	95	96	97	98	99	100

Counting by 1s (Pennies)

1 2 3 4 5 6 7 8 9 10

11 12 13 14 15 16 17 18 19 20

21 22 23 24 25 26 27 28 29 30

31 32 33 34 35 36 37 38 39 40

41 42 43 44 45 46 47 48 49 50

Counting Number Lines

Counting by 5s (Nickels)

5	10	15	20	25	30	35	40	45	50
55	60	65	70	75	80	85	90	95	100

Counting by 10s (Dimes)

10	20	30	40	50	60	70	80	90	100

Counting by 25s (Quarters)

25	50	75	100	125	150	175	200

Play Money

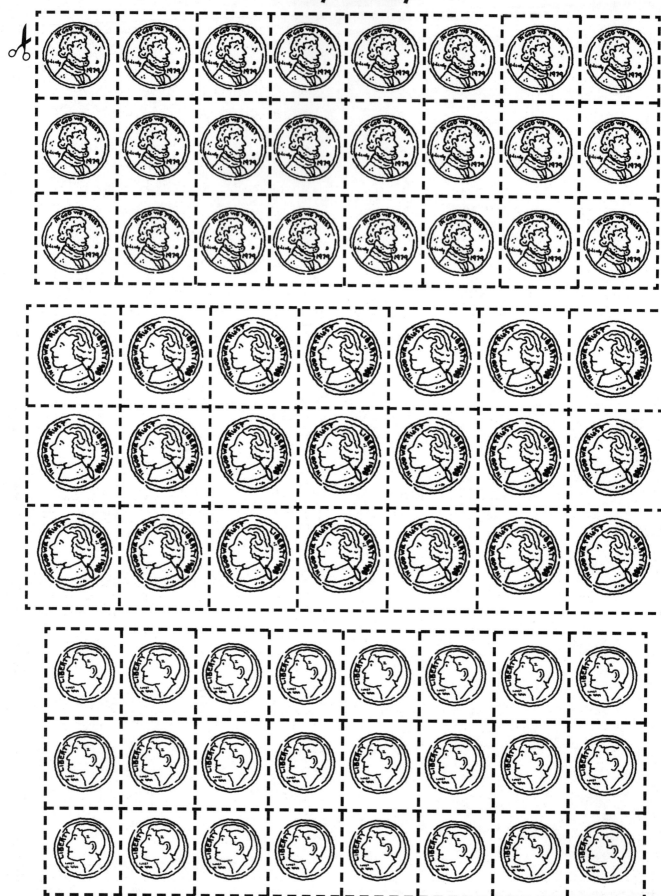

Scholastic Teaching Resources

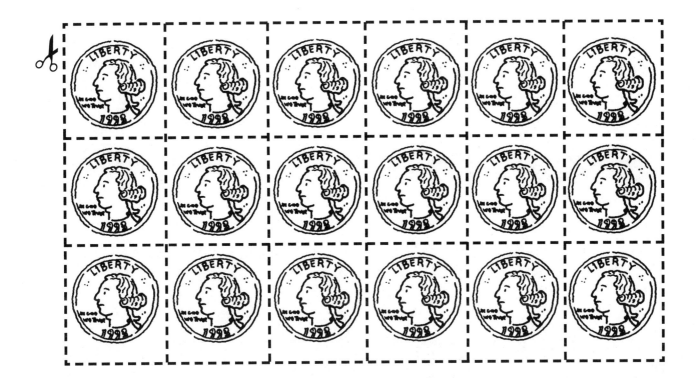

Pennies Payment Form

Name of Item: _____

Price: _____

Color in the number of pennies you need to pay for this item.

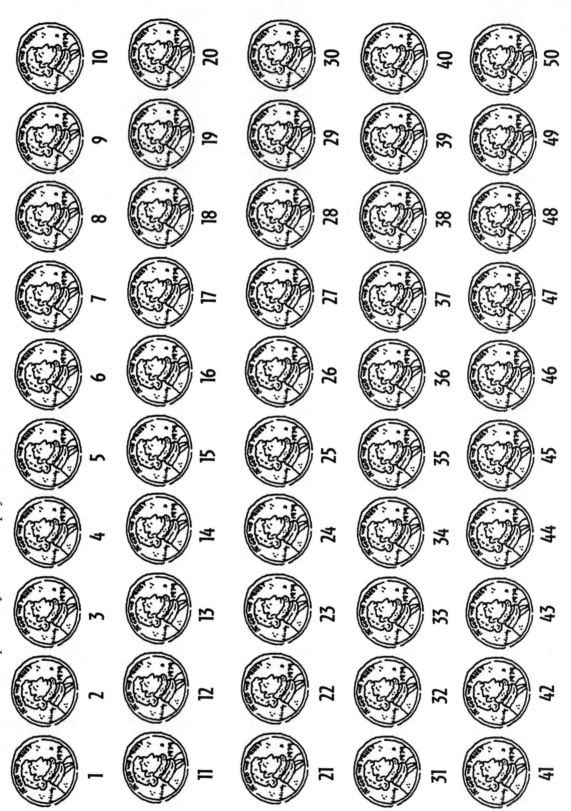

Nickels Payment Form

Name of Item: _____ **Price:** _____

Color in the number of nickels you need to pay for this item.

5	10	15	20	25	30	35	40	45	50
55	60	65	70	75	80	85	90	95	100

Dimes Payment Form

Name of Item: _____ **Price:** _____

Color in the number of dimes you need to pay for this item.

10	20	30	40	50	60	70	80	90	100

Multi-Coins Payment Form

Name of Item: _____

Color in the number of coins you need to pay for this item.

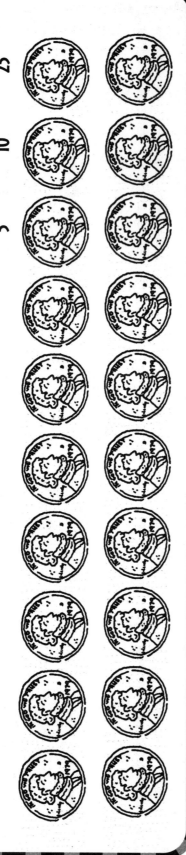

5   10   25

Dollars Payment Form

Name of Item: _____

Price: _____

Color in the number of dollars you need to pay for this item.

1   2   3   4   5

6   7   8   9   10

Best Books Store

MATH SKILLS

- Money recognition
- Number recognition
- Counting
- Writing numbers
- One-to-one correspondence
- Sorting
- Addition
- Subtraction

OTHER SKILLS

- Language and listening
- Sound and word recognition
- Writing words
- Problem solving
- Group cooperation

YOU'LL NEED

- Books *(Ask parents for donations of used books.)*
- Shelves or tables to display books
- "Best Books Store" sign
- Stick-on tags or labels
- Markers
- Hundred Board (page 9) or Counting Number Line (pages 10–11)
- Play money (pages 12–13)
- Payment forms (page 14–16)

Note to Parents

Dear Parents:

We are setting up our "Best Books Store" center, where children will be using play money to buy books. At this math learning center, children will be developing important skills such as writing numbers and words, number recognition, money recognition, sorting, addition, subtraction, and decoding words.

We would very much appreciate it if you could donate used books for our Best Books Store.

Sincerely,

CLASS DISCUSSION

Before setting up the Best Books Store, engage children in a discussion with the following questions:

✔ Have you ever been to a bookstore?

✔ How are the books arranged? Why do you think they are arranged this way? *(Books may be arranged by topics, such as people, animals, sports, and so on. This kind of arrangement makes books easy to find.)*

✔ What do you think people who work in a bookstore do? *(Arrange books, collect money, make sure that there are enough books, and so on)*

✔ What will we need to set up our bookstore? *(Books, prices, sign, money, and people to collect money and organize the books)*

SETTING UP THE CENTER

• Decide where and how you want to set up the Best Books Store. Ask children for suggestions. Using their ideas as a starting point, show children how they might sort books by alphabetical order, by title, by author, or by topic.

• Distribute stick-on tags or labels and markers to children. Decide what the price range should be, then ask children to write price tags for the books. Encourage children to refer to a number line as they write numbers. It's AMAZING how fewer children write backward numbers during this meaningful writing time!

• Have children sort the books on appropriate shelves or tables in the center. You may also want to ask for volunteers to create signs for the shelves and tables.

CENTER TIME

• Assign two children at a time to be the "sellers." One child can collect the money, while the other can bag the items.

• Invite "shoppers" into the bookstore and let them browse through the books.

• If you decide to use payment forms, suggest that children buy one book at a time, fill out the form, and pay the cashier. Children can then shop some more if there's time.

ENRICHMENT ACTIVITIES

Book Tally:

Keep a running tally of the books donated each day. Cross off the number collected on a Hundred chart.

Book Critique Clothespin Chart:

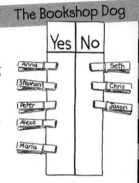

Draw a T-chart on butcher paper and label one side "Yes" and the other side "No" (see right). Choose a book from the bookstore to read aloud to the class. After reading the book, ask children: Did you like the book we just read? Give each child a clothespin and have him or her indicate "Yes" or "No" by putting the clothespin on the chart.

Favorite Scene Card Graph:

Read aloud two books to the class. Distribute large index cards to the class and invite each child to draw his or her favorite scene from one of the books. Display the cards on a bulletin board next to their matching book titles.

Book Patterns:

Invite children to sort the books in a pattern. An example of an "AB" pattern might be red book, blue book, red book, blue book, red book, and so on.

Guess Their Weight:

Challenge children to guess how much 10 small books weigh. What about 10 medium books? 10 large books?

Size Them Up:

Divide the class into small groups. Give each group a number of books and ask them to order the books from smallest to largest.

Multicultural Connection:

If possible, display a variety of books from different countries.

Literature Links

The Bookshop Dog by Cynthia Rylant (Scholastic, 1996)

The Little Old Lady Who Loved to Read by John Winch (Holiday House, 1997)

The Bookstore Cat by Cindy Wheeler (Random House, 1994)

Petunia by Roger Duvoism (Knopf, 2000)

Teddy Bear Clothing Store

MATH SKILLS
- Money recognition
- Number recognition
- Counting
- Writing numbers
- One-to-one correspondence
- Sorting
- Addition
- Subtraction
- Measurement

OTHER SKILLS
- Language and listening
- Sound and word recognition
- Writing words
- Problem solving
- Group cooperation

YOU'LL NEED
- Teddy bear clothes *(These can be used baby clothes that will fit a medium-sized teddy bear. Ask for clothing donations from the school community.)*
- Shelves or separate tables to display clothes
- "Teddy Bear Clothing Store" sign
- Stick-on tags or labels
- Markers
- Hundred Board (page 9) or Counting Number Line (pages 10–11)
- Play money (pages 12–13)
- Payment forms (page 14–16)

Note to Parents

Dear Parents:

We are setting up our "Teddy Bear Clothing Store" center, where children will be using play money to buy clothes for their teddy bears. At this math learning center, children will be developing important skills such as recognizing and writing numbers and words, understanding money, sorting, addition, subtraction, measurement, and group cooperation.

We would very much appreciate it if you could donate any small clothes that would fit a medium-sized teddy bear (used baby clothes work well).

Sincerely,

CLASS DISCUSSION

Before setting up the Teddy Bear Clothing Store, engage children in a discussion with the following questions:

✔ Have you ever been to a clothing store? What do you know about clothing stores?

✔ What do you think we need to set up our Teddy Bear Clothing Store? (*Sort clothes, decide how much the clothes will cost, put price tags on the clothes, and so on*)

✔ What do you think people who work in a clothing store do? (*Arrange clothes, collect money, make sure that there are enough clothes for customers to buy, and so on*)

✔ What do customers need to do? (*Bring money, bring their teddy bears, try clothes on the teddy bears, buy clothes, and so on*)

SETTING UP THE CENTER

• Decide where and how you want to set up the Teddy Bear Clothing Store. Will you have folded clothes set on shelves or tables, or will you hang up the clothes in a rack? Will you display all the clothes at once? If you have small groups taking turns shopping, "choice" items might be quickly sold out. Ask children for suggestions on how to solve these questions. Children often have clever ideas. You'll be surprised at how much you can learn from them!

• Ask children for ideas on how to sort the clothes. Using their ideas as a starting point, demonstrate how they might sort clothes by type or size. Encourage children to create signs to indicate the various clothing areas.

• Distribute stick-on tags or labels and markers, and ask children to write price tags for the clothes. (If you plan to use the payment forms, suggest that children write the name of the items on the price tags so shoppers can easily copy the item name on their payment form.)

CENTER TIME

• Invite children to bring their teddy bears to school. You may wish to keep the teddy bears for a few days to complete all of the center time and extra activities. Join in the children's imaginary world and provide "snacks and blankies" for the teddies' overnight stay.

• If you decide to use payment forms, suggest that children buy one item at a time, fill out the form, and pay the cashier. If there's time, children can come back and shop some more.

ENRICHMENT ACTIVITIES

Button Sorting:

Read "The Lost Button" from *Frog and Toad Are Friends* by Arnold Lobel. Invite children to sit in a circle, then distribute buttons so that each child holds one button. Name an attribute, such as "round," and ask children who have a button with this attribute to stand up. Then name another attribute, such as "white." Ask children who have buttons that are round AND white to remain standing; the rest should sit back down. Continue adding attributes until only a few children remain standing. As a variation, distribute buttons to small groups of children and have them sort the buttons in a Venn diagram.

Bear Sorting:

As children bring in their teddy bears, invite them to sort the bears by one or more attributes, such as size or color.

Measuring the Teddies:

Provide children with string, interlocking blocks, or measuring tape to measure their teddy bears. Children can use string to measure around the waist of their teddy bear. Have them cut the string to the measured length and display the strings on a graph to see how many bears are 12, 13, or 14 inches wide, for example. Use the interlocking blocks to measure the height of the teddy bears. Make a bar graph to display the bears' heights.

Multicultural Connection:

Discuss customary and traditional clothing worn in different countries. This is a good time to display dolls dressed in international costume attire. Any bears dressed in international clothing would be great fun for the children to see!

Literature Links

Jesse Bear, What Will You Wear? by Nancy White Carlstrom (Little Simon, 1996)

Corduroy by Don Freeman (Viking Press, 1968)

"The Lost Button" from *Frog and Toad Are Friends* by Arnold Lobel (HarperCollins, 1979)

A Fair Bear Share by Stuart Murphy (HarperTrophy, 1998)

A Pair of Socks by Stuart Murphy (Scott Foresman, 1996)

The Button Box by Margarette S. Reid (Scott Foresman, 1990)

Rent-a-Pet Shop

MATH SKILLS

- Money recognition
- Understanding quantity of money
- Counting
- One-to-one correspondence
- Sorting

- Number recognition
- Writing numbers
- Addition
- Subtraction
- Division

OTHER SKILLS

- Problem solving
- Group cooperation
- Learning responsibility
  and respect for animals

- Language and listening
- Sound and word recognition
- Writing words

YOU'LL NEED

- Toy pets *(plastic or stuffed fishes, birds, turtles/tortoises, cats, dogs, mice, lizards, and so on)*
- Other pet-store items *(brushes, rocks, yarn balls, small balls, food dishes made from margarine tubs, collars, and so on)*
- Shelves or separate tables
- "Rent-a-Pet Shop" sign
- Pet Care Travel Log (page 30)
- Animal posters *(made by children)*
- Boxes or containers *(Chinese restaurant containers are great for carrying small toy animals home)*
- Stick-on tags or labels
- Markers
- Hundred Board (page 9) or Counting Number Line (pages 10–11)
- Play money (pages 12–13)
- Payment forms (page 14–16)

Note to Parents

Dear Parents:

We are setting up our "Rent-a-Pet Shop" center, where we will have a variety of toy pets (fishes, birds, turtles, cats, dog, mice, and so on) and pet supplies. When your child comes to the center, he or she will "rent a pet" to bring home along with appropriate pet toys and food. Your child may keep the pet and other items for a week. Please help your child care for the toy pet as if it were a real animal.

In addition to learning about how to care for animals, children will practice important math skills such as money recognition, one-to-one correspondence, writing numbers, counting, subtraction, and division. Other skills children will use include problem solving, group cooperation, language and listening, and sound/word recognition. As you can see, there are many educational aspects to this math learning center!

Sincerely,

CLASS DISCUSSION

Before setting up the Rent-a-Pet Shop, engage children in a discussion with the following questions:

✔ Have you ever been to a pet store? What can you find in a pet store? *(Different choices of pets to buy; items needed to take care of the pets)*

✔ What do you think we need to set up a pet store in the classroom? *(Bring in toy animals, containers for pet food, toys and other pet supplies, and so on)*

✔ What do you think people who work in a pet store do? *(Take care of the animals, help customers choose the right pet, give advice about their care, collect money, and so on)*

✔ What do customers do? *(Decide which type of pet to buy, what supplies the pet needs, and so on)*

SETTING UP THE CENTER

• Decide where and how you want to set up the Rent-a-Pet Shop. Ask children to divide each group of animals equally into different containers. For example, they could divide the birds equally into the number of birdcages you have at hand.

• Have children measure out pet food and put them in baggies or empty cans that the children decorate themselves. For example, children might put half a cup of dried dog food into a baggie or can, then decorate the container with a dog's picture. Use this opportunity to discuss what different animals need to eat to stay healthy. You could also challenge children by having them divide a given amount of food equally into available cans. When they're finished, encourage children to find out how many spoonfuls of food are in each can.

• Distribute stick-on tags or labels and markers, and ask children to write labels and price tags for all the items.

CENTER TIME

• You may want to have separate cashiers for the different areas of the pet store. One cashier could collect money at the food area, while another collects money at the pet-supply area.

• If children are using payment forms, suggest that they buy one item at a time, fill out the form, and pay the cashier.

• After children have finished shopping, give each shopper a copy of the "Pet Care Travel Log" in his or her shopping bag. Ask children to fill in the log at home for each day of the week that they keep their pet.

ENRICHMENT ACTIVITIES

Learn More About Pets:

Arrange a field trip to a nearby pet store or invite a veterinarian to speak to your class about pet care. To expand children's knowledge about the world, you might wish to discuss different types of pets found in different countries. Children would be very surprised to know that in some Asian countries, crickets are kept in cages at home. Monkeys and parrots are pets for many people who live in the rain-forest areas. Japan treasures their wonderful carp fish.

Pet Division:

Divide the class into small groups and give each group a number of toy pets, such as 20 mice. Give each group five jars. Ask: How many mice should go in each jar so that each jar has the same number of mice?

Estimating Pet Food:

Fill a jar with dog biscuits and challenge children to estimate how many dog biscuits are in the jar. Put slips of paper and pencils near the jar so children can come and write their estimates on the paper. As an alternative, put fish crackers in a fish bowl and ask children to estimate how many fish crackers are in the bowl. Ask: Which number do you think is closest to the number of crackers in the bowl—15, 50, or 100?

Animal Riddles:

Without showing children, place a toy animal in a mystery box. Recite a riddle about the animal such as: "Is it a fish, turtle, or lizard? It cannot walk."

Grouping Types of Animals:

Discuss with children characteristics of different types of animals, such as mammals, birds, amphibians, or reptiles, and fishes. Then ask children to group the toy pets according to types of animals.

Tangram Pets:

Read aloud *Grandfather Tang's Story* by Ann Tompert. Using the tangrams in the book as models, cut out your own sets of tangrams from cardstock. Distribute the tangrams to children, encouraging them to create a picture of their pet using the tangrams.

Survey Says...:

Encourage children to interview the teachers in your school (or any other group) and ask if they have any pets. Gather children's data and display it in a graph called "Teachers' Pets."

Favorite Pet Graph:

Set out a bunch of old magazines for children to cut out pictures of their favorite type of pet. On butcher paper, create a graph where children can glue a picture of their favorite pet under the appropriate label.

Literature Links

Measuring Penny by Loreen Leedy (Holt & Co., 2000)

The Salamander Room by Anne Mazer (Knopf, 1994)

Moonbear's Pet by Frank Asch (Aladdin Library, 2000)

Arthur's Pet Business by Marc Brown (Little Brown & Co., 1993)

Feathers for Lunch by Lois Ehlert (Voyager, 1996)

Fish Eyes by Lois Ehlert (Harcourt, 2001)

Grandfather Tang's Story by Ann Tompert (Dragonfly, 1997)

How Much Is That Doggie in the Window? by Iza Trapan (Charlesbridge, 1997)

One Fish, Two Fish, Red Fish, Blue Fish (video) by Dr. Seuss (Sony Wonder, 1994)

Pet Care Travel Log

Animal's Name _____

This animal is a _____ (type of animal.)

To keep my pet healthy, I will give my pet lots of attention and love!

Signed _____ (child's name)

	M	T	W	Th	F	Sa	Su
I fed my pet.							
I cleaned my pet's living area.							
I groomed my pet.							
I exercised my pet.							
Other:							

Write about your experience with your pet. What did you do with your pet? Where did your pet stay? Did you have any fun adventures with your pet? (Parent: Please help your child write his or her responses below. Then ask your child to draw a picture of the pet.)

Gift Shop

MATH SKILLS

- Money recognition
- Counting
- One-to-one correspondence
- Sorting
- Number recognition
- Writing numbers
- Addition
- Subtraction

OTHER SKILLS

- Problem solving
- Group cooperation
- Writing words
- Language and listening
- Sound and word recognition

YOU'LL NEED

- Gifts (*You may want to ask parents for donations.*)
- Tables
- "Gift Shop" sign
- Stick-on tags or labels
- Markers
- Bags
- Hundred Board (page 9) or Counting Number Line (pages 10–11)
- Play money (pages 12–13)
- Payment forms (page 14–16)

Note to Parents

Dear Parents:

We are setting up our "Gift Shop" center in the classroom. To supply our shop, we would appreciate donations of any small gift items. The children will be purchasing gifts at the center for themselves, siblings, friends, or mom and dad. For this reason, any donation of gifts appropriate for children or adults would be very much appreciated. We thank you for any contribution you can make!

While at this math learning center, children will be practicing important skills such as money recognition, understanding quantity of money, categorizing, group cooperation, problem solving, language and listening, and sound/word recognition. The children are very excited to begin learning at this center!

Sincerely,

CLASS DISCUSSION

Before setting up the Gift Shop, engage children in a discussion with the following questions:

✔ What do you know about a gift shop?

✔ Why do you think people buy gifts? *(To get someone something he or she needs, to make someone happy, to celebrate a special occasion, and so on)*

✔ How should we set up our Gift Shop center? *(Bring in gifts, arrange them, and display them nicely)*

SETTING UP THE CENTER

• Decide ahead of time which type of payment process you will be using. This could affect how you will set up your center and how you label items.

• Ask children for ideas on how to sort the gift items. One suggestion is to sort them according to price; one area could have all same-priced gifts. This type of setup lends itself to easy selection and direct payment.

CENTER TIME

• Paying directly with money is always a choice in the payment process. If you wish to use a payment form, have shoppers buy one item at a time, fill out the form, and pay the cashier.

ENRICHMENT ACTIVITIES

Estimating Volume:

Ask children to estimate how many interlocking cubes will fit in a particular gift box. Fill the box with interlocking cubes to see how many fit inside.

The Traveling Box:

Send a gift box home with a child and ask the child to put an item in the box and return it to class the following day. Challenge the rest of the class to guess what's inside the box. The child could offer hints as to what's inside until someone guesses correctly. Give the box to another child to bring home.

Gifts From the Heart:

Reinforce the concept that giving doesn't always have to be in the form of a material gift. Showing love and kindness to each other is also a gift. Ask children: How could you show love and kindness to other people? List children's responses on a chart. Don't forget to add a few of your ideas, too! For example, children might suggest going to a senior center to sing songs or presenting a play to parents. Encourage children to do

kind deeds for others and invite them to draw a picture of and write about their deeds. At the end of the month, place all the pictures in a class book labeled "Caring Kids—A Gift of Kindness." Let the class book travel from home to home.

Journal Writing:

After children have visited the Gift Shop, ask them to write in their journal about the gift they purchased. Who is the gift for? Why did they buy this particular gift for the person?

Beginning Sound Bar Graph:

Ask each child to choose a gift from the Gift Shop. On the floor, place large cards with some letters of the alphabet. Have each child put his or her gift under the appropriate beginning sound.

Literature Links

The Giving Tree by Shel Silverstein (HarperCollins, 1986)

Mr. Rabbit and the Lovely Present by Charlotte Zolotow (HarperCollins, 1990)

The Mother's Day Mice by Eve Bunting (Clarion, 1988)

A Chair for My Mother by Vera B. Williams (Scott Foresman, 1984)

Uno, Dos, Tres, One, Two, Three by Pat Mora (Houghton Mifflin, 2000)

Claude, the Dog: A Christmas Story by Dick Gackenbach (Houghton Mifflin, 1984)

Grocery Store

MATH SKILLS

- Money recognition
- Number recognition
- Counting
- Writing numbers
- One-to-one correspondence
- Sorting
- Addition
- Subtraction
- Weights and measurement

OTHER SKILLS

- Language and listening
- Sound and word recognition
- Writing words
- Problem solving
- Group cooperation

YOU'LL NEED

- Food items (*empty food containers, such as boxes of cereal, rice, and pasta, milk cartons, juice bottles, egg containers, as well as plastic fruits and vegetables*)
- Shelves or tables to display items
- "Grocery Store" sign
- Stick-on tags or labels
- Markers
- Grocery bags
- Weighing scale
- Rulers or other measurement sticks
- Hundred Board (page 9) or Counting Number Line (pages 10–11)
- Play money (pages 12–13)
- Payment forms (page 14–16)

Note to Parents

Dear Parents:

We are getting ready to set up our "Grocery Store" center in the classroom. To supply our center, we would appreciate any donation of empty but clean containers such as cereal boxes, small milk cartons, jam jars, margarine tubs, and egg cartons. Using a dark marker, please circle the words indicating the product name on the container (for example, "milk" or "eggs"). This will help the children know what words to write on their payment form.

In this math learning center, children will be practicing important skills such as money recognition, understanding quantity of money, weighing and measuring items, categorizing, group cooperation, problem solving, language and listening, and sound/word recognition.

The children are excited about this center! We thank you for any contribution you can make.

Sincerely,

CLASS DISCUSSION

Before setting up the Grocery Store, engage children in a discussion with the following questions:

✔ What do you know about a grocery store? *(It's a place that sells a variety of foods and other items.)*

✔ What do you think people who work in a grocery store do? *(Group items on the shelves, check out and bag foods, help customers find items, and so on)*

✔ How should we set up our Grocery Store? *(Group items on the shelves, have a place to check out and bag foods, and so on)*

SETTING UP THE CENTER

• Most likely, you will receive MANY empty packages and containers. Make the sorting process an EASY ONE! Assign each child a particular item, such as an egg carton, and give that child a sample of the item. As you go through the donations, hold up each item and ask who has other items similar to the one you're holding. Then give that child the item to hold.

• Distribute stick-on tags or labels and markers and ask children to write price tags for the different items.

• To help children who will be filling out payment forms, circle the product's name on each container for their easy reference. I've actually asked parents to do this *before* they send in the item.

CENTER TIME

• For children who are using a payment form, encourage them to select one or two items at a time. (Limit to one item for younger children.) Have them fill out their form, then pay for the items. Put the payment form in their bagged groceries as proof of payment. This shopping process can be repeated again and again.

• After each group has finished shopping, ask for volunteers to help restock the shelves for future customers.

ENRICHMENT ACTIVITIES

Learn More About Groceries:

Take the class on a field trip to a nearby grocery store. Or invite a grocer to speak to your class about his or her job.

Playing House:

After children have finished shopping at the Grocery Store, have them bring their groceries to the "house center." Encourage them to sort their items and place them in the appropriate areas. Ask: What items need to go in the cabinet, refrigerator, freezer, and so on?

Inventory Math:

Ask children to stock each shelf with a specific number of items; for example, 10 items. After a day of selling, have children count how many items are left in each shelf. Ask: How many more items do you need to restock each shelf so that it will have 10 items?

Measuring Fruits and Vegetables:

Bring in different fruits and have children weigh each item on a scale. If a fruit weighs almost the same as one cube, for example, its cost could be one dime. If a fruit weighs near two cubes, the cost could be two dimes, and so on. Display the "Counting by Tens (Dimes)" chart (page 11) for children to use as reference. Children can also use a ruler to measure carrots and potatoes. If a vegetable measures close to one inch, its cost could be one dime, and so on. (Variation: Use other amounts of money, such as a penny for younger children or a quarter for older children. Make sure you display the appropriate skip-counting chart for children's reference.)

Pyramid Food Chart:

On a large piece of butcher paper, draw the pyramid food chart and place it on the floor. Invite children to sort grocery food items by placing them in the correct category on the pyramid food chart.

"Money Saved!" Coupon Game:

This game is perfect for small groups of three or four players. Collect food coupons and place them in a stack between the players. Players take turns picking a coupon from the stack. Each player reads aloud the amount of money on the coupon. This is his or her "money saved." Players continue taking turns until all the coupons are gone. Each player adds up his or her "money saved." The player with the most money saved wins!

Price Comparison:

Give a child three to five food items that are marked with prices. Ask the child to place them in order from least expensive to most expensive. Have him or her write down the prices in order on a piece of paper.

How Much More?

Fill two different-sized jars with uncooked rice. Have children predict which jar holds more rice. Then encourage them to check their answer by using measuring cups and/or spoons. As a challenge, ask children: How much more rice does one jar hold than the other?

Weighty Items:

Provide children with different grocery items to weigh and compare against a sample item. Give children three plates: one plate is labeled "lighter," another "heavier," and the last the same." Have children weigh the items and put them on the appropriate plates.

Make a Commercial:

Invite groups of children to make and present a commercial to persuade people to buy their products!

Fruit and Vegetable Prints:

Cut fruits and vegetables (such as apples, carrots, and potatoes) in half. Provide tempera paint and construction paper, plus newspapers to protect the table surface. Have children dip the cut fruit and vegetables in paint and make prints on paper.

Favorite Food Venn Diagram:

If you have some available, hula hoops are great for this graphing activity. Otherwise, use yarn or string to make large, overlapping circles on the floor. Label one circle "I like HOT DOGS" and the other, "I like PIZZA." Give each child a slip of paper on which to write his or her name. Then ask children: Do you like hot dogs, pizza, or both? Have children place their names in the appropriate area. Explain that if they like both types of food, they should put their names in the overlap.

Multicultural Connection:

It's easy to find foods from other countries. Bring in food items that children may see, touch, and taste! Point out food from different countries in the grocery store. Consider letting children create a toy vehicle from vegetables, just like children from Haiti sometimes do!

Literature Links

Pass the Fritters, Critters by Cheryl Chapman (Simon & Schuster, 1993)

Potluck by Anne Shelby (Orchard, 1991)

Each Orange Had Eight Slices by Paul Giganti Jr. (Mulberry, 1999)

Just Enough Carrots by Stuart Murphy (Scott Foresman, 1997)

The Berenstain Bears Get the Gimmies by Stan & Jan Berenstain (Random House, 1988)

Post Office

MATH SKILLS

- Money recognition (nickels)
- Number recognition
- Counting by 5s
- Writing numbers
- One-to-one correspondence
- Sorting
- Addition
- Weighing

OTHER SKILLS

- Language and listening
- Sound and word recognition
- Writing words
- Problem solving
- Group cooperation

YOU'LL NEED

- Half-gallon milk cartons, one for each child in the class
- Large shoebox
- Envelopes, assorted sizes
- Weighing scale
- "Post Office" sign
- Stamps
- Stamping tool (to cancel stamps)
- Paper and pencils
- Chart with words and/or sentences children can copy for their letters
- Hundred Board (page 9)
- Counting by 5s Number Line (page 11)
- Play money (pages 12–13)
  - Payment forms (page 14–16)

Note to Parents

Dear Parents:

We are setting up our "Post Office" center in the classroom. The children will be practicing important skills such as money recognition (nickels), understanding quantity of money, counting by fives, number recognition, addition, weighing items, categorizing, group cooperation, problem solving, language and listening, and sound/word recognition.

In addition, children will participate in a graphing experience using stamps. Please send in any canceled stamps you may have. Thank you for any contributions you can make.

Sincerely,

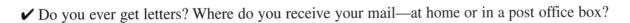

CLASS DISCUSSION

Before setting up the Post Office center, engage children in a discussion with the following questions:

✔ Do you ever get letters? Where do you receive your mail—at home or in a post office box?

✔ What are some items that arrive in the mail? *(Letters, magazines, packages)*

✔ What do you need to do when you want to send a letter? *(Write the letter, place it in an envelope, address the envelope, put a stamp on the envelope, and put the letter in a mailbox)* Take this opportunity to help children to learn their own personal address.

✔ How does a letter get from the sender to the person it is addressed to? *(By truck, train, or plane)* Discuss the sequence of events needed to get a letter from one place to another.

✔ How can we set up a post office in the classroom? *(Write letters, put stamps on envelopes, sort the mail, bring mail to where it needs to go)*

SETTING UP THE CENTER

• Make a mailbox for the class using a large shoebox. Label the box "Class Mailbox."

• Guide children to make mailboxes out of half-gallon milk cartons. Invite children to decorate their own mailboxes and write their names and house numbers on them. Have children line up the mailboxes in alphabetical order.

• Assign an area where stamps will be sold, as well as an area where stamps will be canceled (on letters received in the class mailbox).

CENTER TIME

• Encourage children to write letters to friends or family members. You may want to display a chart of sentences and/or words that children can copy. Have children put their letter in an envelope and address the envelope.

• The cost to mail a letter (the number of stamps needed) could depend on its size. (See chart at right.) Children buy stamps to put on their letters.

• Explain to children that each stamp costs 5 cents. This way, children count by fives (nickels) as they buy stamps for their letters. Display the "Counting by 5s" number line for children to use for reference. (NOTE: You may want to adjust prices according to children's skill level.)

HOW MANY STAMPS FOR EACH ENVELOPE

• Have children drop their stamped letters in the Class Mailbox. Assign a postal-office worker to check the mail in the Class Mailbox: Does each letter have enough stamps? Is it addressed correctly? If yes, the postal-office worker should mark the envelope "canceled" then deliver it to children's individual mailboxes.

ENRICHMENT ACTIVITIES

Learn More About the Post Office:

Take children on a field trip to a nearby post office. Or invite a postal worker to speak to your class about his or her job.

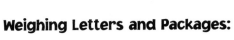

Weighing Letters and Packages:

Children can weigh letters and packages in two ways:

1) If you have a two-sided weighing apparatus, children can put the letter or package on one side and cubes on the other side. Each cube represents one stamp. For example, if a letter weighs two cubes, it needs two stamps.

2) If you have a weighing apparatus with a dial indicator, weigh the letter or package as usual. When the dial moves to a number or close to a number, use that number to indicate how many stamps the letter or package needs. For example, if a letter weighs close to the number 3, it would need three stamps.

Counting Stamps:

As children bring in canceled stamps, write a math story to indicate how many more stamps are received each day. For example: "On October 1st, we had 5 stamps. We got 4 more today. How many do we have? 5 stamps + 4 stamps = 9 stamps"

Another way to keep track of the number of stamps you collect is by crossing off a box on the Hundred Board each time you get a stamp. You can also do these activities with the letters children put in the class mailbox.

"More or Less Than" Stamp Chart:

Divide a large piece of butcher paper in half. Label one side "More Than 5 Cents" and the other, "Less Than 5 Cents." Distribute canceled stamps to the class. Ask children: Is your stamp more or less than 5 cents? Invite children to come up one at a time to chart and glue their stamps on the correct side.

Multicultural Connection:

Children will find stamps from other countries very interesting. If possible, establish a pen-pal relationship with a school from a different country.

Literature Links

Never Mail an Elephant by Mike Thaler (Troll, 1994)

Harvey Hare, Postman Extraordinaire by Bernadette Watts (North South Books, 1997)

The Jolly Postman by Janet and Allan Ahlbery (Little Brown, 2001)

A Letter to Amy by Ezra Jack Keats (Puffin, 1998)

The Post Office Book: Mail and How It Moves by Gail Gibbons (HarperTrophy, 1986)

Post Office Stamps

Super Sticker Store

MATH SKILLS

- Recognition of money
- Counting
- One-to-one correspondence
- Sorting
- Number recognition
- Writing numbers
- Addition
- Subtraction

OTHER SKILLS

- Problem solving
- Group cooperation
- Writing words
- Language and listening
- Sound and word recognition

YOU'LL NEED

- Stickers
- Shelves or separate tables
- Containers *(to sort stickers into groups)*
- "Sticker Store" sign
- Hundred Board (page 9) or Counting Number Line (pages 10–11)
- Play money (pages 12–13)
- Payment forms (page 14–16)

Note to Parents

Dear Parents:

We are setting up our "Super Sticker Store" center in the classroom. In this math learning center, children will be practicing important skills such as money recognition, understanding quantity of money, categorizing, group cooperation, problem solving, language and listening, and sound/word recognition.

Sincerely,

CLASS DISCUSSION

Before setting up the Super Sticker Store, engage children in a discussion with the following questions:

✔ Have you ever been to a sticker store?

✔ What do you think we need to set up a sticker store in the classroom?
   (Sort stickers, put them in containers, price each group of stickers)

SETTING UP THE CENTER

• Ask children for ideas on how they might sort the stickers. Using their ideas, have children sort the stickers into the containers. Label each container with the category in which the stamps belong. (This is a great time to utilize all those leftover stickers you may have collected over the years!)

CENTER TIME

• Invite children to come to the store to shop for stickers. Children can pay for the stickers with play money or use the payment forms.

• Have cashiers count the money as they collect it.

ENRICHMENT ACTIVITIES

Sticky Math Problems:

Invite children to write a math problem using the stickers. A sample problem might be written as: 3 animal stickers + 2 people stickers = 5 stickers.

Sticker Collection:

Give children their own nametags to wear for a week. For every small success a child achieves, award stickers for the child to put on his or her nametag. At the end of the week, have children count the stickers they have collected.

You could also turn this into a graphing activity. Children could graph how many of each type of stickers they received.

Sticker Story:

Give each child ten stickers. Invite children to make up a story using some or all of the stickers. Have them write their story and use the stickers to "illustrate" their story.

Category Venn Diagram:

Give children stickers to sort according to categories, such as animals, plants, and so on. Show children how to create a Venn diagram by drawing two overlapping circles and labeling them according to the categories they have. Then have children place the stickers under their proper categories.

Size Bar Graph:

Have children sort stickers according to size—small, medium, and large. Then have them create a bar graph showing how many stickers belong in each size.

Literature Links

My Sticker Dictionary by Carol Osterink (Learning Horizons, 1992)

Count With Little Bunny by Harriet Ziefert (Viking, 1994)

Basil Bear Goes on a Trip by Marilyn Woody (Gold'n'Honey Books, 1998)

Flower Shop

MATH SKILLS

- Money recognition (nickels, dimes, quarters)
- Number recognition
- Understanding quantity of nickels, dimes, and quarters
- Writing numbers
- Counting by 5s
- One-to-one correspondence
- Sorting
- Addition

OTHER SKILLS

- Language and listening
- Sound and word recognition
- Writing words
- Problem solving
- Group cooperation

YOU'LL NEED

- Green pipe cleaners
- White paper squares, assorted sizes
- Flower pattern (page 53)
- Colored markers
- Scissors
- Shelves or tables to display flowers
- Vases *(water bottles work well)*
- "Flower Shop" sign
- Large container of dirt *(for the farm area)*
- Counting by 5s Number Line (page 11)
- Play money (pages 12–13)
   - Payment forms (page 14–16)

Note to Parents

Dear Parents:

We are getting ready to set up a "Flower Shop" center in the classroom. Children will be making their own flowers using colored markers, paper, and green pipe cleaners.

As they work in this math learning center, children will learn some important concepts, such as money recognition (nickels, dimes, and quarters), understanding quantity of money, counting by fives, categorizing, group cooperation, problem solving, language and listening, and sound/word recognition.

Sincerely,

CLASS DISCUSSION

Before setting up the Flower Shop, engage children in a discussion with the following questions:

✔ What do you know about flower shops? *(They sell flowers, vases, and so on.)*

✔ What are some occasions when people might send flowers? *(Holidays, special events)*

✔ Where does the flower shop get the flowers? *(They can grow their own flowers or get them from flower growers.)*

✔ How can we arrange the flowers and other shop items for sale? *(Group flowers by kinds or create beautiful arrangements)*

✔ How can we set up our class's flower shop? *(Make flowers, sort and label them, put them in vases)*

SETTING UP THE CENTER

• Collect large display vases for grouping flowers. You'll also need several plastic water-bottle vases for customers to use to bring their flowers home. (A vase is given with every purchase. The shopper can decorate the classroom with the vase of flowers.)

• Invite children to make 30 flowers for the store opening. Give each child a white paper square and some markers. Ask children to draw a flower on their square (just the bloom without the stem), then stick a green pipe cleaner into the paper flower.

• Ask children for ideas on how to sort the flowers in the large display vases. You may want to demonstrate different ways to sort flowers. Display the flowers in the large display vases.

CENTER TIME

• Before opening the Flower Shop center, explain to the class that some children will get to be the **OWNERS** of the flower shop business and others will be the **FARMERS** who sell flowers to the flower shop. Explain each group's role:

FARMERS: Establish a "farm area" with a large container of dirt and several pipe cleaners stuck in the soil. The farmers color flower blossoms and stick them on the pipe cleaners. Each farmer makes 10 flowers to sell to the Flower Shop. The flower-shop owner pays the farmer 10 nickels. The farmers can then use their nickels to buy other flowers in the flower shop.

OWNERS: While the farmers make the flowers, the shop owners sort the flowers in their shop. Encourage shop owners to invent names for the flowers and label the vases with the flowers' names and prices. Prices could be 5 cents, 10 cents, or 25 cents. (You may want to ask children to put a picture of the coin on the vase to indicate the price.) If they have time, shop owners can decorate vases and decorate the shop with pictures. When the farmers are ready, the owners buy the farmers' flowers for 5 cents each. In turn, the farmers use this earned money to buy "flower shop" flowers. The owners put the flowers in vases for the farmers to bring home.

ENRICHMENT ACTIVITIES

Pressed Flowers:

Demonstrate to children how to press flowers and preserve them for a very long time. Pick some flowers from the garden (violets and buttercups are good examples). Get a thick dictionary or phone book and place the flowers in the middle of the book. Leave them in there for a few weeks. Later, children can use the flowers on cards or as part of a picture.

Flower Seeds Mosaic:

Invite children to draw a picture on paper. When finished, show them how to brush a thin layer of glue inside the lines. Then have them sprinkle the area with flower seeds to create a beautiful mosaic.

Planting Time:

This activity is best done in the early spring. Bring in enough paper cups and soil so that each child could have his or her own "flower pot." Plant flower seeds in the containers and show children how to mist the soil with a spray bottle to keep it damp. Discuss how different plants grow. Invite children to predict which plants will sprout first, then make a class graph that shows which plants appeared first. When the plants start to grow, encourage children to measure and record the growth of various plants.

International Garden:

Wouldn't it be fun to start an international garden? If your school has a garden, grow foods and flowers that originated from or are associated with other countries or regions. For example:

- Peru – tomatoes
- Iran – spinach
- Italy – zucchini
- Mexico – tomatillos
- South Africa – geraniums
- Netherlands – tulips
- China – bean sprouts
- Middle East – rose, coriander
- Scandinavia – dill
- Central America – avocado

Flower Color Bar Graph:

Ask students: What is your favorite color of flowers? Make copies of a simple flower pattern (page 53) and distribute to children. Invite each child to color the flower with his or her favorite color and place it on a graph next to its appropriate label.

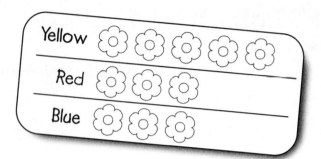

Garden Flower Venn Diagram:

If you live in a suburban area, you might have children create a Venn diagram showing which flowers grow in their gardens. On a chart, draw two large overlapping circles. On the right circle, write the name of a flower, such as "daisies." On the left circle, write the name of another flower, such as "roses." In the middle of the chart, where both circles overlap, put the word "Both." Give each child a flower pattern to place in the appropriate circle.

Literature Links

Planting a Rainbow by Lois Ehlert (Harcourt, 1992)

The Tiny Seed by Eric Carle (Aladdin, 2001)

The Carrot Seed by Ruth Krauss (BT Bound, 1999)

The Magic School Bus Plants Seeds by Patricia Relf (Scholastic, 1995)

Jack's Garden by Henry Cole (Mulberry, 1997)

Over Under in the Garden by Pat Schories (Farrar Strauss Giroux, 1996)

Flower Pattern

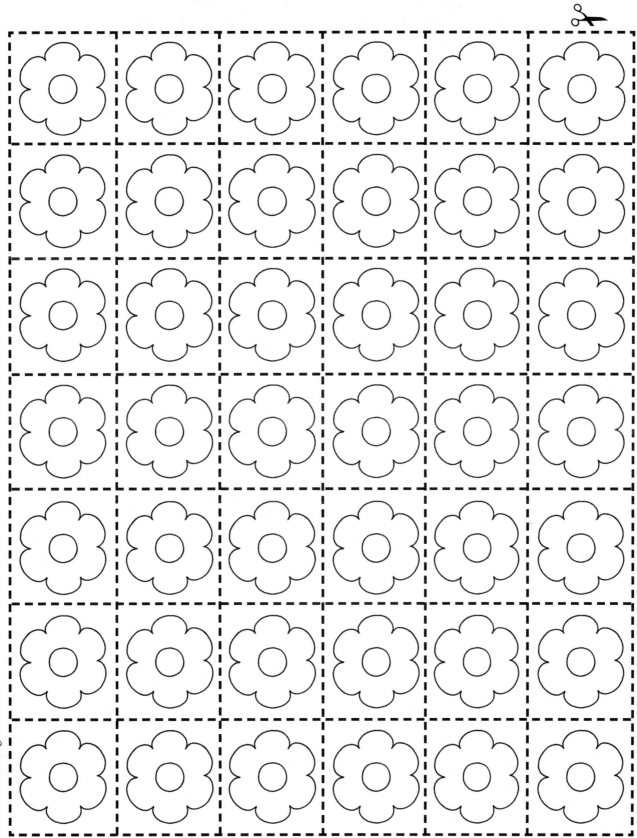

Lemonade Stand

MATH SKILLS

- Money recognition (nickels, dimes, quarters)
- Number recognition
- Understanding quantity of nickels, dimes, and quarters
- Writing numbers
- Counting by 5s, 10s, 25s
- One-to-one correspondence
- Sorting
- Addition
- Subtraction

OTHER SKILLS

- Language and listening
- Sound and word recognition
- Writing words
- Problem solving
- Group cooperation

YOU'LL NEED

- Tables
- Lemonade *(You can make this in class or ask parents to bring some in already made.)*
- "Lemonade for Sale" sign
- Paper or plastic cups
- Lemonade Stand Money Mat (page 58)
- Counting Number Line (pages 10–11)
- Play money (pages 12–13)

Note to Parents

Dear Parents:

The children will have the opportunity to set up a "Lemonade Stand" center in the classroom! We will be making lemonade in the classroom, then selling it for refreshment (using play money, of course).

Some concepts children will learn in this math learning center include money recognition (nickels, dimes, and quarters), understanding quantity of money, counting by fives, tens, and twenty-fives, categorizing, group cooperation, problem solving, language and listening, and sound/word recognition.

Sincerely,

CLASS DISCUSSION

Before setting up the Lemonade Stand, engage children in a discussion with the following questions:

✔ Do you know anyone who sold lemonade at a lemonade stand?

✔ What do you think we need to set up a lemonade stand? *(Make lemonade, make a sign, have someone collect the money, another person to give out the lemonade)*

SETTING UP THE CENTER

• With the class, estimate how much lemonade will be sold. Ask children: How many cups do you think we'll need?

• Decide who will provide the lemonade to be sold. Will it be made by the class, purchased at a store, or sent in by parents?

• Create signs showing how much each glass would cost.

CENTER TIME

You may have students who are ready to use different denominations of coins. If so, this center would be excellent practice!

• Lemonade costs 25 cents a cup. Customers buy the lemonade using nickels, dimes, or quarters. (If necessary, adjust prices to meet your students' mathematical abilities and needs.)

• The Lemonade Stand Money Mat (page 58) can be a helpful tool for children who are selling lemonade. When a child accepts money for one glass of lemonade, he or she puts the money on the Money Mat to see if the correct amount has been given.

Literature Links

Good Lemonade by Frank Asch (Franklin Watts, 1976)

Lemonade for Sale by Stuart J. Murphy (HarperCollins, 1998)

ENRICHMENT ACTIVITIES

Lemon Prints:

Cut lemons in half and place them next to cups of paint. Invite children to dip the lemon halves in paint to create print art. If you are having an outside lemonade stand, consider displaying the children's artwork nearby!

Lemon Print Graph:

Ask children: What is your favorite food made with lemons? Create a chart or graph labeled with children's top three choices (for example, lemon pie, lemon pudding, and lemon cake). Cut a lemon in half. Have each child dip the lemon in yellow paint and make a print on the graph next to his or her choice.

Seed Bar Graph:

Challenge students to find out how many seeds lemons have. Have children work in pairs and count the seeds in a lemon. Have them glue the seeds on a piece of paper. When everyone is finished, invite children to glue their paper on the appropriate spot on a graph.

Counting Lemon Seeds	
Less than 5 seeds	🍋🍋🍋
6 to 10 seeds	🍋🍋🍋
More than 10 seeds	🍋🍋

Lemonade Stand
Money Mat

25

5   10   15   20   25

10   20   25

10   15   20   25

It's a Small World Eatery

MATH SKILLS

- Money recognition
- Understanding quantity of money
- One-to-one correspondence
- Sorting
- Number recognition
- Writing numbers
- Addition
- Subtraction

OTHER SKILLS

- Problem solving
- Group cooperation
- Cultural awareness
- Language and listening
- Sound and word recognition
- Writing words

YOU'LL NEED

- Tables *(for customers and for the cooking area)*
- Pretend food *(Children can draw food on cardboard or think of creative ways to represent it.*)*
- Dishware *(Use paper rolled inside plastic cups to represent various drinks.)*
- Menus *(Invite children to make them.)*
- "It's a Small World Eatery" sign
- Hundred Board (page 9) or Counting Number Line (pages 10–11)
- Play money (pages 12–13)
- Menu payment form (page 63)

* Children can create pretend food items as suggested below:

Fortune cookies – Make paper fortune cookies and write a sentence on a strip of paper to insert in each one. Children could give these (or real fortune cookies) to customers as they leave the eatery.

Chow mein – Glue real chow mein on cardboard.

Spaghetti – Glue real spaghetti on cardboard.

Tacos – Use burlap for tacos and yellow rubber bands for cheese.

Sushi – Cut a long rectangular piece of a white sheet. Roll this with paper lettuce and fish inside.

Note to Parents

Dear Parents:

We are getting ready to set up our "It's a Small World Eatery," a multicultural restaurant learning center. We will be selling pretend foods from around the world. Children will be making and serving the foods. Some of the skills children will be using at this math learning center include money recognition (nickels, dimes, and quarters), understanding quantity of money, counting by 5s, 10s, and 25s, categorizing, group cooperation, problem solving, language and listening, and sound/word recognition.

Sincerely,

CLASS DISCUSSION

Class discussions at this time should always include how valuable all people are in this world. Emphasize that every person is unique and special in his or her own way. Point out how much richer we all are for knowing each other. It would also be very interesting for children to know that many of our toys, food, clothing, and other important items come to us from people of other countries!

Before setting up the "It's a Small World Eatery," engage children in a discussion with the following questions:

✔ What foods have you eaten that came from other countries? *(Children may not be aware that some of the foods they like to eat come from other countries; for example, pizza from Italy, tacos from Mexico, noodles from China, and so on)*

✔ Where have you eaten multicultural foods? *(Restaurants or maybe at home)*

✔ What do you think we need to do to set up a multicultural restaurant? *(Make the food and price it, make a menu, set up tables and chairs for customers to sit on, take customers' orders, and serve them food)*

SETTING UP THE CENTER

- Ask children for ideas on how to create food for this center. Group the foods according to what country or region they came from.

- Ask children to label and price the food items. We suggest pricing the foods at 5, 10, or 25 cents.

- Set up tables and chairs where "customers" can sit and eat. (You may also want to make a "Please wait to be served" sign as well.)

CENTER TIME

- Assign some children to be the waiters or waitresses, and others to be the customers. (Children can switch roles, if desired.)

- The fun begins! Customers take their Menu Payment Form and choose from the food items on the main table. They fill in their forms to indicate their selections and give them to the waiters or waitresses. They then return to their tables to wait for service. (If you want, you can provide customers with coloring-book pages to color as they wait, the way some restaurants do.)

- The waiters or waitresses serve the food ordered and collect the money afterwards.

ENRICHMENT ACTIVITIES

Decorations From Around the World:

Invite children to decorate the eatery with items that represent various cultures. Ask children to bring in items from home or make items such as Chinese lanterns; Mexican piñatas, placemats, and tissue flowers; Japanese carp drawings or paintings. Children can also make flags from different countries using colored construction paper. Or they can "dress up" paper dolls to represent their own cultural heritage.

Favorite Food Triple Venn Diagram:

Ask children: What is your favorite multicultural food? On a chart, draw three overlapping circles and label them with the top-three most popular answers. For example, students may say Chinese, French, and Italian. Distribute small sticky notes on which children can write their names. Then ask children to come up one at a time and stick their names in the appropriate circle.

Cultural Heritage Bar Graph:

Ask children: What cultural heritage does your family belong to? (Some children may have more than one cultural heritage. Let them decide which culture they relate to the most.) List children's answers, then create a bar graph to reflect all their answers.

Literature Links

Hands Around the World by Susan Milord (Williamson Publishing, 1992)

Uno, Dos, Tres, One, Two, Three by Pat Mora (Houghton Mifflin, 2000)

Saturday Market by Patricia Grossman (Lothrop Lee & Shepard, 1994)

Joining Hands With Other Lands (The Food Song) CD by Jackie Weissman (Kimbo Educational Audio, 1993)

Menu Payment Form

Write Food Item

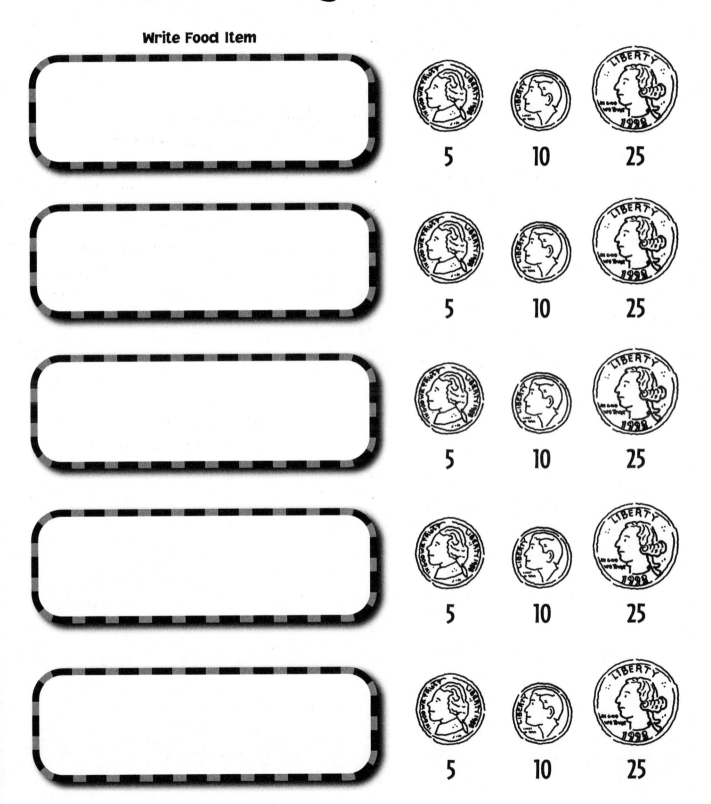